This Book Belongs To:

Stacey Hart

The Rand McNally Book of
Favorite
Stories of Jesus

by Mary Alice Jones

Rand McNally & Company · Chicago

Established 1856

Library of Congress Catalog Card Number: 81-50278

CONTENTS

THE BABY JESUS

Bible text used: Luke 2:4-8; 1:31b

Mary and Joseph were going to Bethlehem. Mary was riding on a little gray donkey. Joseph was walking, leading the donkey.

Soon it would be dark. Mary was tired. She knew it was time for her baby to be born. She drew her shawl closer about her to keep warm.

"There," Joseph said. "There is Bethlehem. It is not far now."

Mary looked up and saw the town. "We are almost there," she said.

Mary and Joseph came to the town. They went to the inn where travelers stayed. The door was closed.

Joseph knocked at the door. He
knocked again and again.

The inn keeper opened the door. He held up his lantern. When he saw that a traveler was there he shook his head. "We have no room left," he said. "The inn is full."

"But what can we do?" Joseph
asked. "Mary is very tired. She will

soon have a baby. I must find a place
where Mary can be warm and rest."

The inn keeper sighed. "I want to help you," he said. "But so many people have come tonight. There is a stable back of the inn where we keep the cow. It is warm. There is straw for a bed. There is no other place. I will lend you a lantern."

Joseph wanted a nicer place for Mary. But Mary smiled. "It is all right, Joseph," she said. "We will be warm in the stable. We can have a straw bed."

So Joseph led the donkey to the stable. And Mary got off the donkey and went into the stable.

Joseph hung the lantern on a peg. He made a straw bed for Mary. He put his long cloak over her. As Mary rested, Joseph fed the donkey.

Mary was warm in the stable. The donkey and the cow were warm.

Outside it was cold. The little town of Bethlehem was quiet. Everyone was in bed.

Everybody was asleep. Then Mary woke up. Joseph woke up. Mary knew that soon she would have her baby. And before daylight came, the baby

was born. Mary wrapped the tiny
baby in the soft clothes she had
brought.

Joseph said, "He is the loveliest
baby in all the world, Mary."

Joseph went to the door. He saw
stars and stars and stars in the sky.
They had never seemed so bright. Far
away he seemed to hear happy voices

singing. Joseph turned to look at Mary and the baby. "Even the skies seem to be happy tonight, Mary. The skies seem to be glad about your baby."

Mary held the baby close. No one, not even Joseph, could know how happy she was. "His name will be Jesus," she said.

Joseph said, "His name will be Jesus."

And Mary sang a little song to the baby Jesus. And outside, the bright stars shone and the happy voices sang.

JESUS AND THE CHILDREN

Bible references used:
MATTHEW 11:16, 17; 18:1-4; 19:13-15;
MARK 9:36, 37; 10:16; LUKE 18:15, 16

Jesus liked children. One day he was working in the carpenter shop. He looked out of the window. Some children were playing. He stopped his work and stood at the door and watched. He smiled. The children smiled. They knew Jesus liked them.

Jesus wanted children to be happy. He wanted people to be good to them. He was glad when he saw mothers and fathers taking good care of children.

One day, Jesus heard some children singing. They were making music on a little flute. They were singing and dancing to the music. Jesus listened. He liked to hear the children's music.

Another day Jesus was talking with some big people. He was telling them about God. A little boy was there.

Jesus saw him. He called, "Come, little boy. Come near to me." And the little boy came to Jesus.

The little boy knew Jesus liked him. He was not afraid. Jesus put his arm around the little boy. Jesus told the people, "This little boy knows

that God loves him. And he loves God.
You will all be happier if you love God
and trust him as this little boy does."

Another time Jesus and his friends were traveling. A big crowd of people followed them. Jesus' friends were pleased. They wanted a big crowd to hear Jesus.

In the town some children heard
that Jesus was coming that way. They
wanted to see Jesus. They wanted

to talk with Jesus. They asked their
mothers, "Will you take us to see
Jesus?"

The mothers smiled. They knew
their children wanted to see Jesus.
They wanted to see Jesus, too. They

said, "Yes, we will take you to see Jesus." And they started along the road.

The mothers and the children walked and walked. Then they saw the crowd of people. A little boy called,

"There, look! There are the people.
That is where Jesus is. Let's hurry!"

The mothers and the children came to the edge of the crowd. "How can Jesus see us?" a little girl asked. "There are so many big people."

One of the mothers said, "I see one of the friends of Jesus. I will ask him to help us get through the crowd."

The mother spoke to the friend of
Jesus. But he was not glad that the
children had come. He spoke crossly,

"Don't you see that Jesus is busy?
Important people are here. Take the
children back home."

Then Jesus looked toward the children. He saw what was happening. He left the crowd and came toward the children. He smiled.

Jesus said to his friend, "Never send the children away. I always want them to come to me. God loves them and wants all of us to love them and take care of them."

Then Jesus came to the shade of a tree. He called the children to him. He took the littlest ones up in his arms.

The bigger ones stood close to him.
And Jesus talked with the children.
Jesus liked children.

JESUS WHO HELPED PEOPLE

JESUS AND A SICK CHILD

JAIRUS pushed his way through the crowd. He was almost running, though he looked very tired. He had to find Jesus. He had to find him right now.

Now, Jairus was an important man in the town where he lived. The people liked him and listened when he spoke. But as he came hurrying toward Jesus, Jairus did not look like an important man. He was in trouble, and needed Jesus.

"Please," he called out as soon as he was near enough to be heard, "please come help me. My little girl is very sick. The doctors say they can't help her." Jairus wiped the dust from his face. "You know how to help sick people. Please come."

Just then some people came looking for Jairus. "Do not trouble Jesus to come," they said. "No one can help the little girl now." Jairus was afraid. He thought his little girl had died.

Jesus put his hand on Jairus' shoulder. "Don't be afraid. I will come."

Jairus turned quickly toward his home with Jesus by his side.

When they came to Jairus' house, there were many friends and relatives there. They were crying. Jesus spoke to them. "Do not cry. The child is not dead." But they did not believe him.

So Jesus told the people to stay outside. He knew crying people would not help. Then Jesus went with the mother and daddy into the little girl's room.

How still she lay! Jesus went close to the bed. He stood quietly for a moment looking at the little girl lovingly. He thought of the mother and

daddy who were so sad. He thought of God who loved them all and wanted them to be well and happy. He knew that God was there with them. Jesus took the little girl's hand in his. He spoke gently. "Child, wake up."

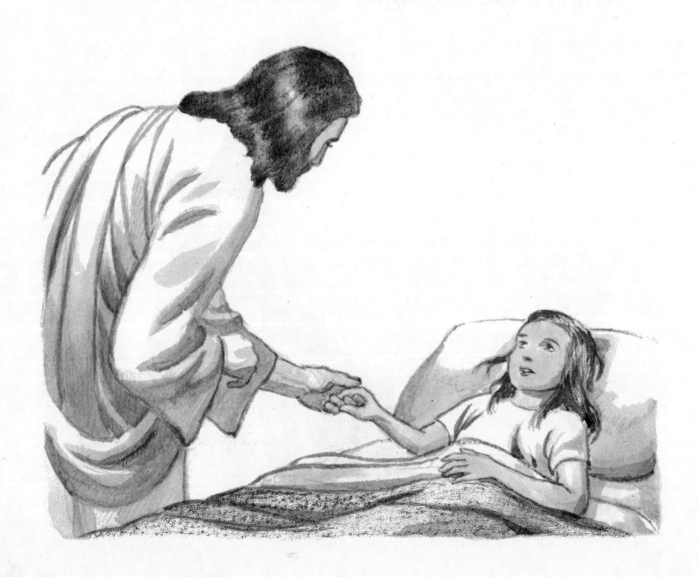

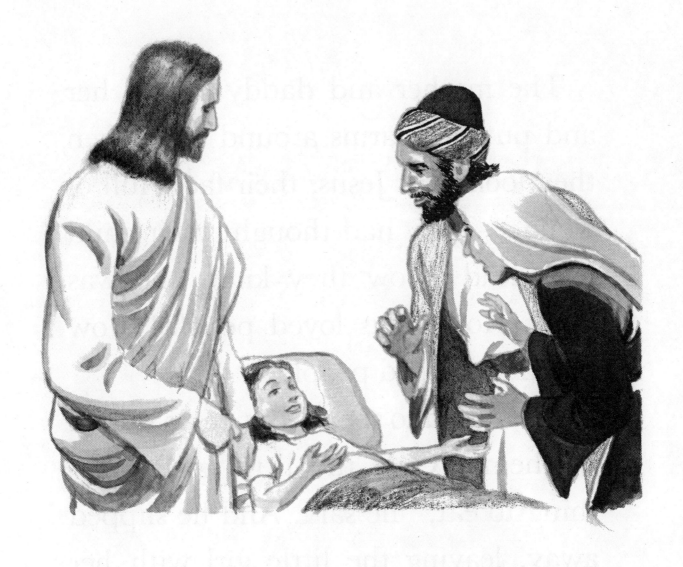

The little girl opened her eyes. She saw the kind face of Jesus. She knew he was helping her. She felt better!

She saw her mother and daddy. She smiled at them. Then she spoke. "I'm hungry," she said.

The mother and daddy ran to her and put their arms around her. Then they looked at Jesus, their faces full of wonder. They had thought their child was dead! Now they knew she was alive. How Jesus loved people! How much he helped people!

They tried to speak. But Jesus smiled at them. "Give the little girl something to eat," he said. And he slipped away, leaving the little girl with her mother and daddy.

A MAN WHO WAS LONESOME

MATTHEW was lonesome. He had no friends. He sat in his office thinking. "Nobody likes me," he thought. "None of the friends I had talk with me any more. They do not invite me to come to see them. They look the other way when they see me coming."

Matthew knew why his friends had stopped liking him. He knew it was because he was working for the Romans. His friends hated the Romans. The Romans had won a war. Now they ruled over Matthew's people. They were angry because the Romans made them pay taxes.

They talked about Matthew. "Matthew has turned against his own people," they said. "He works for our enemies, and he cheats." So Matthew was lonesome as he sat in his office thinking.

Just then Matthew saw someone at his door. He looked up expecting to see a scowling face. Instead, he saw a friendly face. It was Jesus.

Matthew had heard Jesus teach. Now Jesus had come to see him! As Matthew looked at Jesus, he was ashamed of all the wrong he had done. He wanted to be good. He wanted to help his people instead of cheat them.

Then Jesus talked with Matthew.

Jesus knew that Matthew wanted to be good. He said, "Come, Matthew. Leave what you have been doing. Come, be one of my helpers."

How good it was to have someone want him! How good it was to have

someone trust him! Matthew knew that Jesus could help him be the good, friendly man he wanted to be.

So Matthew left his office and went with Jesus. And he became a good friend to his people.

HELPING ANGRY MEN UNDERSTAND

JESUS and his friends did not have any horse or car to use when they traveled. They had to walk from one place to another even when it was far.

One day they were walking along the road toward the big city of Jerusalem. They went through a part of the country where the people did not like travelers to Jerusalem. They thought those who went to Jerusalem were their enemies. As Jesus and his friends walked, it grew late. It was a long time since they had had anything to eat. They needed a place to eat and a place to spend the night.

"I will go ahead and find a place," one of Jesus' friends said. So he ran ahead of the others toward the town.

After a little while he came hurrying back. His clothes were torn. He was very angry.

"They will not let us stay in the

town," he shouted angrily. "See, they hit me. They drove me out of town."

The other friends became angry, too. "It is a wicked town," James said. "A town that will not give travelers something to eat and a place to stay at night is a wicked town."

John turned to Jesus. "Let us ask God to send down fire to burn up the wicked town," he said.

Jesus shook his head. "You do not understand. God does not want us to hurt people. He wants us to help."

John was still angry. "But, teacher,

we need something to eat and a place to stay. They are wicked."

"Yes, John. Come, let us go on farther. We will find food and a place where we can stay." Then he smiled at his angry friends. "But not by burning down the towns," he said.

So they went on to another town. They found food and a place to stay.

FRIENDS WHO WERE AFRAID

JESUS and his friends were in a boat. They were going across a big lake. The water was calm. The friends knew how to sail the boat.

Jesus went to the back of the boat. He was tired. Soon he went to sleep. The boat sailed on.

Then suddenly everything changed.
The sky turned black. The wind blew
hard. The calm sea became full of
roaring waves.

The water dashed over the sides of
the boat. The men were afraid.

One of the men called to Jesus, "Teacher, we are in a bad storm! The boat may sink! Help us!"

Jesus woke up. He looked at the roaring waves of the lake. "Peace! Be still," he said. He looked at his frightened friends. He spoke quietly. "Why are you afraid? Have you no faith? God is with you."

As quickly as it had come, the storm passed.

The wind was no longer howling about them. The waves were no longer pounding the boat. The men went back to work sailing the boat. But they wondered.

"Jesus is different from anyone else," one of them said to another.

"Yes, Jesus is different. The lake is quiet now."

The friend thought a minute. "Yes. And we feel quiet, too. We aren't afraid any more. Jesus helps us when we are afraid."

FRIENDS OF JESUS

FRIENDS WHO HAD A BOAT

SIMON PETER and Andrew were brothers. They had a boat, and fished in the big lake near their town.

One morning Simon Peter and Andrew were working by the shore, getting their nets ready to go fishing. As they worked, some people came to the lake shore. Then more and more people came.

"Why are so many people coming to the lake?" Simon Peter asked.

"There must be some special reason," Andrew answered. "They aren't coming just to see fishermen work!"

"I'll find out," Simon Peter called, as he sprang out of the boat and ran toward the people.

Then he stopped. He saw Jesus in the midst of the crowd. Now he did not have to ask the people why they were there. He knew. They were following Jesus, the new teacher. Simon Peter had heard wonderful things about Jesus. He wanted to know more. So Simon Peter stood still for a moment, watching.

The people were crowding around Jesus. They looked at him as if they trusted him and wanted to hear every word he was saying. Jesus was telling them about God. "God loves each one of you," he said.

As Simon Peter watched, more people came. Now Jesus was very near the lake. The water was back of him. In front of him the little beach was full of people. There was no more room.

Simon Peter went back to his boat. "Jesus, the new teacher, is here," he told Andrew. "The people are coming to hear him."

Andrew stood up in the boat. He wanted to see Jesus, too. "Look! The little waves are lapping about his feet. If any more people come, Jesus will have to wade out into the lake."

"Let's ask him to stand in our boat," Simon Peter said.

Andrew nodded. "Yes, let's do that. We want to help him."

So Simon Peter made his way through the crowd to Jesus. "Teacher," he said, "Andrew and I have a boat. If you will get into the boat, we will row you out a little way. Then more people can hear you." He looked at Jesus' sandals, covered with water. "And you won't get wet," he added.

Jesus looked at his sandals, too. He had

not noticed that they were wet. Then he smiled at Simon Peter. "That is a good plan. It will help."

Andrew had the boat ready. As soon as Jesus stepped into it, the two fishermen rowed out a little way. Then they held the boat steady near the shore.

The people saw Jesus get into the boat. At first they thought he was going away. They looked sad.

Then they saw Jesus standing up in the boat while Simon Peter and Andrew held the oars steady. Now they knew what had happened! Their faces were happy again as they settled down on the little beach. They liked listening to Jesus talk with them from the boat!

Andrew and Simon Peter listened, too. And they became friends and helpers of Jesus.

A FRIEND THE OTHERS DID NOT LIKE

ONCE THERE was a rich man named Zacchaeus. Now Zacchaeus had a fine house
and fine clothes and money to buy anything
he wanted. But he did not have any friends.
His neighbors did not like him. They did
not invite him to their parties. And though
he had much better food than they could
afford to buy, they did not go when he asked
them to dinner.

"Everybody knows that Zacchaeus cheats," the neighbors said. "He always takes more than his share. He is a bad neighbor."

And so Zacchaeus stayed by himself in his fine house.

One day Jesus came to the town where Zacchaeus lived. Now, Zacchaeus had heard

about Jesus. He had heard about the way Jesus had helped sick people be well and how he had helped sad people feel happy again. "Maybe he can help people who are lonesome, too," Zacchaeus thought to himself.

So Zacchaeus ran out to see Jesus. But many people were already standing along

the way. Zacchaeus was not tall. He could not see over the crowd. No one offered to make a place for him. Zacchaeus felt that he *had* to see Jesus! There was a tree by the road. Zacchaeus climbed the tree and sat in the fork of the limbs.

Just then Jesus passed by. He looked up. He saw Zacchaeus. The neighbors saw him, too, and began to laugh and make fun. But as Jesus looked into Zacchaeus' face, he knew that the man was lonely. Jesus' voice was friendly. "Come down, Zacchaeus. I would like to go home with you today."

Zacchaeus could scarcely believe what he had heard. Someone wanted to be friends with him! Someone wanted to come to see him! Scrambling down from the tree, Zacchaeus stood by the side of Jesus, feeling happier than he had felt in a long time. And Jesus and Zacchaeus walked away together toward Zacchaeus' house.

But the people standing by were angry. "Why does Jesus go to Zacchaeus' house?" they asked one another. "Doesn't he know Zacchaeus is a bad neighbor? Doesn't he know Zacchaeus cheats?"

But Zacchaeus was talking with Jesus. Being with Jesus made him ashamed of what he had done.

"I am sorry I have not helped people in my town who are hungry and cold," he said. "I am sorry I have taken more than my share." Jesus was quiet, listening. He

knew that Zacchaeus needed to do more than just to say he was sorry. Zacchaeus knew it, too.

"I will give half of all my money to help people who are hungry," he said. Still Jesus was quiet. Zacchaeus knew he must do even more. "And I will pay back all I have taken unfairly," he said. "Yes, I will give back four times as much as I have taken."

Jesus looked at Zacchaeus as a loving person looks at a friend. He knew that Zacchaeus really was sorry.

"From this day on, Zacchaeus, you will love people and help them. You will be fair instead of cheating. You will not be lonesome, for the people will know you are a good neighbor."

And what Jesus said came true.